# The Kindness Approach
## Written by Nick Yarris

Pablo Picasso was quoted as saying that the *meaning* of life is to find your gift. He also was said to have claimed that the *purpose* of your life is to give that gift away.

Ever since I read that quote, I have found so many meanings to this one simple concept of our lives. You do not have to be an artist to live your life in this way, as the gift of who you actually <u>are</u> is the one gift that you need to most believe in and share.

It is in this fashion that I am now writing this book, as writing this work has become a such central part of the purpose to my own life.

For that one single act alone of writing, there is no greater honor in life. It is such an empowering effort to share this written work with the world as my own art. I do it all so that others learn from my life. That is all I am able to ask of anyone taking time to read this book.

I believe that if you follow some simple instructions which I practice each day, that you too can handle anything life throws at you. No matter what, *this* is the way back from it...

When I got out of prison after 8057 days on America's "Death Row", after being falsely convicted of murder and rape that DNA science later exonerated me of, "I" began.

This is the book that explains how I managed to walk directly from a level-5 Maximum security prison cell, to then start a life of complete freedom. Since release from a 6 foot by 9 foot cell, I have not had one single psychiatric counseling session. I have not needed in all of these 13 years of my freedom.

I need no one to hold my hand and guide me through my tough moments in life. I am the one who leads myself through it all.

Why? Because I took the **"Kindness Approach"** and it worked.

I have shown through an adopted set patterned behavior, a formulated way to not only handle life's most difficult events, but to thrive and grow from them in wondrous ways which you never thought possible.

And before we begin:

I am not a holder of one single educational certificate. I have no qualifications on paper of any sort. I did not finish basic high school and all of my education came through an autodidact effort. It was done while I was in solitary confinement for 23 years in a prison cell no less. I want this to be known before we go on.

I do not pretend to be anything more than one of the finest examples of a well read lay-person who has put perspective on my life. All of it is given to me from my voracious appetite for learning that has allowed me many "life managing tools" to rely upon now.

Because I made clear to all that I have no paper to hang in a frame on a wall does not in any way invalidate this work. This work is not based on my scholastic achievements alone, rather it is my ability as a writer to show that my daily practices are the basis of a Neuro Plasticity healing in my brain. I will then show how I have mastered my past traumas from life just by using this meticulous effort.

In other words, it really does not matter that my name in has no PhD. at the end of my title. I know fully what I propose as true and is further provable within these pages that I now follow on with.

I will show how anyone, regardless of education level, can become just as clever at managing life as anybody else they meet, all from just practicing my methods.

In this work I will rely upon various studies and also further use the like minded points of views of others like myself, who have found this way of healing from the "brain training" we employ daily. From daily prayers, to feeding others, or listening to music, there is no end to the many ways physically that you can re-wire your brain. This effort is then the core basis to re-shaping every part of your outlook on life. It really is that simple.

And finally, I am going to share with all, how my efforts are now currently affecting, or have previously impacted others directly. I will share how they too have changed things personally from my showing them my skills. Many of which are things that they never before believed possible for themselves to master or overcome.

I have used these tools to develop a charisma so empowering that I above all others truly have found a way to like myself as I interact with humans.

I really thrive off of the wonderful energy that I share with other people in this way. I went from a man who was once so sure that all my life would always be pure sorrow, to now triumphantly having "everything".

Thank you for opening this book and reading my words. I promise you that if you go a bit further, that this book will change your life forever. It is up to you for that to be a really meaningful gift, or just a passing moment of no real regard. It has taken me 13 years to hold this perspective now which I share. It has been a very challenging accumulation of my work and I truly hope you can appreciate it all. I sure do.

# We all have healing capabilities

My own way of learning to heal my brain began in my very first days of my freedom in 2004. I was instructed to sit down beside my mother Harriet "Jayne" Yarris, who's home I was first living in upon release. My mother informed me that she had something very important that she wished to share with me.

At 74 years of age as we sat together in her home on Elmwood Avenue in Philadelphia that day, I looked at the loving face of the one person who truly paid the highest emotional price for my incarceration. I was sitting before her just as I was in her home having dinner with her on December 15th 1981 when a murder happened 25 miles away. I would be convicted of that murder despite the incredulous realization she held that she was with me when it occurred.

•

I knew that she had some really deep things worrying her and as I patiently waited for her to gather herself, I knew also that I was going to be pliant and sweet to whatever she had to offer up for me to consider.

Holding my hand tenderly in hers, then taking a breath as she looked me in the face, my mother began:

"Nicky, I have something very important to say to you and I want you to really *listen* to what it is that I have to say".

Once I had assured my mother of my complete willingness to pay heed to her words, she then told me:

"I need you to be a *nice* man Nicky. I need you to be a *very* polite man. I need you to always say 'Yes Ma'am' and 'Yes Sir' to adults when you speak"

. I looked at my mother and I knew that there was more to follow so I sat quietly.

Harriet Jayne Yarris straightened me right up with what she then said, which was:

"I also want you to be especially polite and respectful to women because **all** of this madness happened to us as a family because you told a lie to try and get out of a lie."

I was hit by her words like water hissing on a fire. I was so well aware that I had put myself in the way of the criminal charges that led to my going to Death Row. It was my lie about knowing information about an unsolved murder case, when I didn't, that had ruined my life.

I knew fully as she spoke, how it was indeed only by my own my actions that my misfortune was shaped in life. I was never to forget that by my trying to barter for my freedom from trumped up charges that were originally falsely laid on me to begin with by police, that I had started this. I undid any hope for justice by my own hand. I knew what she meant. It hurt deeply but it was needed to be said.

My mother explained to me that if I was *not* a polite man and if I did *not* do as she asked me to do, that it was a complete waste of everyone's time for me to have come home from jail.

As her words sunk in, I swore fervently inside that I was going to honor her one wish.

I was going to go out each day and make the real effort to be as kind and humble as possible, all that all the while yet being truly engaging and harmonious with others.

I took my mother's words as mantra. I set forth with nothing more than an ambition to just try and focus each day on being very positive about my interactions with others in my daily life. This one set behavior became like a challenge to me in a physical sense. Instead of a gym to build muscles, I was using my daily interactions in life to build my self up.

I had no idea these actions are the very building blocks to *Neuro Plasticity*.

I did not at first recognize the way my brain was being daily rewarded chemically from my actions. I just knew that I was feeling so much better each time that I went into a business and made the staff smile and laugh. I knew nothing of the way my brain was mending as I played with children and animals, or when I went into nature to appreciate it's calming effects.

With my eyes shut and falling face forward, I dove deeply into my mothers wishes of me. I saw myself as a beacon of good that was able to draw others to me in like minded ways, all for how I presented myself to them. As I projected both empathetic caring and genuine love, I was also feeding my brain all of the energy to which it grew.

Within months of trying this daily effort to be super polite and openly gregarious, I felt so much changing within me. I allowed my mother to shave off my hair and I refused to wear a hat any longer so I felt free to smile.

I then began taking myself serious enough to start an international speaking campaign all across Europe to fight capital punishment in Pennsylvania by using embargo of trade and economics as my platform.

In October of 2004, just 9 months after I was set free from a maximum security prison cell, I was standing in the halls of Governments and held the utmost attention of elected officials or world leaders. I knew one thing for certain as I spoke in those moments that were either in London, Rome, Paris, or Stockholm: I would have never gotten there by having anger own me. I knew my kind ways and polite mannerism had opened every door for me to get there.

I have to admit here that I have an advantage over a lot of other people in life because of one thing: I was formerly living in a place of confinement where your words were guarded for how they could get you killed.

I lived in a place where, if you had a vocal outburst with someone, it was the prelude to violence. I learned on Death Row that there are no "frivolous words" when your very life depended on *how* and *what* you said in the face of others around you.

So yes, through the most dire of settings I learned how to curb my words for my ability to survive. And still, this is now your lesson to embrace for how this one point is so true: There are no frivolous words in life and what you say and how you say things is so utterly important to your well being.

I know this to be further true for how I worked for a long time to learn *how* to speak to myself. Yes, speaking to yourself is so important! How else can you find the will to empower your ID? My assuring you that speaking aloud to yourself is not only NOT the act of a "crazy person", but is instead the act of the sanest person you could be.

My belief in this all comes from this one perspective I that I now share here:

At the age of 22 I took one photograph of myself and I began to quietly, and with as much caring nature to my voice as I could find, I spoke to myself. I decided to use my voice to be the one soothing feature to my day. Since I was in isolation in prison, I had to learn how to have a way to encourage myself not to self harm or give in to anger.

At first it felt so odd doing this act which we laugh at others for doing in public. Yet soon enough, I looked forward to telling myself how many wonderful aspects of myself that I liked. I did well to make sure that when I spoke to myself that I did so in the sweetest of tones. I used every effort to be as empathetic without a single pitying mannerism to it all as well.

It was my being able to speak to myself that helped me handle my teeth broken in my mouth from the guards beating me brutally.

I sat in my cell alone and I cared for myself as if I was caring for a loved one. I dealt with having my face crushed by steel capped boots, as well as other serious trauma to my body, all by soothingly nourishing the sweetest feelings for myself. I then began an effort driven by how I spoke in oh so caring ways to my own battered reflection.

Instead of an ego driven narcissism, this act each day of speaking to my reflection became the basis of a strength that drove me. The more I became the biggest supporter of Nick Yarris, the man whom I knew inside, the more that I felt like nothing said *or* done to me could ever touch my spiritual being.

Day in and day out I talked to myself in loving ways and I told myself that none of this could own me if I found a way to "forgive them" for what they did to me. How? How could I figure out this one thing that tests so many of us?

I forgave them to *dismiss them* from my mind.

Complete dismissal of the relevance to another person is the hardest punch you can swing. Completely forging in your mind that some person matters so little to you that their acts hold no feelings to you inside is the act of forgiveness to...YOU!

You see, the notion that you have to struggle to forgive someone else is your ego telling you that your suffering is so great that they need to hold this place of hate inside of you.

That seed of hate is far more destructive to your growth than it is to them in so many ways. If you hate someone in life, they own you. They own what your mood is going to be when you think of them and they own the deterioration of your own health that you hand over to them daily.

When I recognized this truth, I no longer attached this huge significance to what we call "forgiveness".

I saw that as long as I was able to completely dismiss someone either from my life, or my feelings towards them, that I was actually being emotionally kind to myself. I saw that when I spared myself angst or upset over another, how instead of being hurt over the memories of what someone did to me, I was smiling. I was smiling at how much I cared about myself enough to treat my own self so kindly so as to not let them hurt me further. I became very proud of myself for how I simply let anything from yesterday go away, all for how I was seeing it as an act of being good to myself.

Yes, I fell in love with the man that I am now from speaking so beautifully to myself in prison. I took this one gift home from that time in my life and I now use it daily to make any hurts from others all hold such little significance, that these people end up hurting inside for not being able to hold any meaning to me.

Trust me,when you can completely mentally blank someone and go right on being happy, it is the biggest empowerment you can feel over them.

Then there is this last bit that I thrive off of in thought: I always know that no matter what, not one person who has harmed me in life now lives a better life than I do. They are in no way as loving or good to their loved-ones as I am. They can never be as selfless, kind, or treat anyone better than I do.

I know that anyone who is no longer in my life can never hold a notion of being empowered over me in that I proved myself to be better than they are, and I go on daily showing it. Just that alone is enough for me to move on...

And once again I see this is how your brain feeds off of this positive thought process so that the next time someone acts poorly, you have set forth the per-scenario help for your emotional strength dealing with it later.

You will actually be many times better at handling things once you handle the first one as I showed my perspective above.

By this point in my life, I promise you, my readers of this work, that no one can get me to lose composure emotionally. I have faced every imaginable social scenario that others in the "free world" face daily since my release from prison. Each time that I have used my methods of prep-perspective and post-event evaluations, it has worked to spare me angst.

I have not one single person in my life whom I actually hate. I am so free in this one way because not one person can sit quietly feeling sly for how they know I lament or self inflict hurtful thoughts over them. Instead, they sit in befuddlement at how I am such a happy person who is so willing to continue to believe in all that I do about the rest of humanity.

Again and again Neuro Plasticity is growing and building me up because I keep trying so very hard to be forgiving of myself, just for trying sincerely to encourage my kindest responses to life's idiots or hurtful people.

What this all taught me is that as long as I continued to put myself out there, I was getting so much more than self confidence, I was growing a mindset that put me in the best possible position moving forward when things did go badly.

This behavior directly translated into my dealing with my daily challenges in life which are not related to others humans as well.

When I first got out of jail I had no resources to get medical treatment. I hadn't any way to get help with housing or employment because the state wanted me to just fade away.

My ability to approach all of this huge social disadvantage, was by first not taking this all so *personally*.

I did not want to be trapped having the view that *I* was being unfairly treated in a singled out fashion. This helped me see a way past it all by not attaching too much to what I was denied or losing out on in contrast to what any other person got in life that I did not.

Instead of using every negative before me as a crutch to lament things in life, I just kept being very kind and sweet in the face of it all.

Because of my medical issues acquired in prison that led to my asking to die for a crime I did not commit, I was told that I was going to need a liver transplant to live upon release.

I was told initially that my life was going to be severely shortened due to what was done to me in 23 years of imprisonment. I heard this even before I got to enjoy any of my freedom.

I accepted this news about the projections of my health knowing that the only thing that I could actually do to help myself was to be as stress free as possible.

If I chose to allow this dim view of my future to own my outlook, I had no hope. I knew that I was cheating myself out of enjoying whatever time I had outside of prison walls if I did this.

So, just like being faced with others that hurt me in life or who have harmed me mentally, I decided to be very willing to be nice and pliant in the face of this huge challenge. I decided to then do every little act that I could think to do to heal my body with food, prayer and simple exercise. I chose to just be super subtle to all around me and sweetheart-like to myself and to others I interacted with in every form.

Within six months of release from prison my body reacted to this stress free loving and nurturing so much so, that I was completely healed of Hepatitis-C infection.

I took no medications and I did nothing more that eat healthy foods, pray each day and be super polite as I tried exercise to build my body.

My beautiful brain did the rest.

# The Way I lived has led me to you

Ever since those first few days of my freedom, when my mother asked me to be kind, I was living in a manner that was the only good way to do it. I saw early and often how this would allow me to have anything relevant to share later on in life.

I had to go through every human emotion, I had to go through all of the ups and downs we all face, and I had to experience each part of it with my reflecting in every chance given who I was for it. I became a better me for it all. Trust me when I tell you that I truly have paid my dues in this area of it all. I not only faced all of the personal challenges post-incarceration holds, but I also had to deal with some very low acts being done to me from others in my life. I have also had incredible amounts of tragedy befall me and this too has really been a test.

Without lament about one single bit of this, nor for purposes other than to just give you a thumbnail outline of what I am hinting upon, here goes what I had to deal with since release:

Going in reverse...

A month before I began this book my newborn child Jaymie Leigh died in her cot. I found her dead after a 40 minute nap. I was the first human and the last human to hold this child.

I have a film documentary that is now out world-wide on "Netflix" titled "The Fear of 13". Millions of people have watched this film and have written me so many amazing messages while the director who made this film has robbed me of money he promised me for making this film. They have completely used me and yet I deal with it without revealing to watchers of the film the hurt it should cause me because that would cheat them of my film's message.

Prior to this I spent the previous year before this book was written being homeless and living on the streets. I had given 6 years of my life to my last partner, and she decided that her need of me was gone overnight once she met some guy in a bar. She felt that I had earned nothing for my many years of kindness to her. In the end, she stole what was left of my money and left me to fend for two small dogs, living in the streets of Los Angeles.

Again, I did not allow humiliating hurts ruin me. I simply went on to find another to whom I could show my best self to now in Laura.

Before this happened I had my now 10 year old child stolen from me by my $2^{nd}$ wife, whom I married when I first got released from prison. This person used the courts in the UK to ruin my bonds with my child and I have not seen my own daughter for nearly 4 years as I sit here writing this.

Before this happened I was robbed many times for the money given to me from the state of Pennsylvania for wrongful imprisonment. I have had every type of con game run on me by others. Each time they saw my kindness as my weakness and they stole from me.

And each time I determined that only one real thing was to come out of it all was this: NO ONE was going to take my kind nature from me. I looked at it this way: Not one of the people who has wronged me in life can carry themselves in life as I do now because they sold me their worth in their actions.

I honestly believe that as long as I never surrender my kindness to anyone, I am never going to fall prey to being as they are.

Lastly, each day of my life I suffer agonizing physical pain from the un-treated broken bones left to me from many beatings in prison. I also have 2 collapsed discs in my neck from a work injury causing me agony daily.

I also have a detached retina in my eye that causes me to have blinding headaches daily. (courtesy of steel capped boots kicking my face in)

My point to sharing all of this hardship history is that though I may live in pain so severe that it would buckle most humans, I have reminded a nice man. I do not go around in a foul mood and project my pain on others. Instead, I am actually even kinder to others in empathy for how lucky they are to not suffer as I do.

I know that I could use any one of these burdens life holds for me as an excuse to be both bitter or feeling like I am owed something from life. I know that I could claim my many years of suffering as a way to excuse bad behavior too. And for all of that, I would be a complete hollow shell of a man. If I know anything valuable from this whole ordeal it is that pain and hurt are as as much a part of making us grow as is the joy and glee we crave.

What would my life be without the pain that made me so grateful? I simply see all of the horrible things done to me as a "toll" that was asked of me by God to pay in my life. And with each toll paid in full, I feel as though I have the right to smile in gratefulness to live beyond it.

I actually am thankful that the many terrible things that have befallen me have somehow actually happened to *me*, as the thought of some other human having to put up with it all simply would break my heart in empathy for them.

What I am trying to achieve in this way of sharing my path in life to this point of this book, is simply so that you the reader can see how this book has little to do with my past life in prison. These are the issues that we all face.

If you live in society today you have the same troubles as many will. If they are truly crushing as many of mine were, then it is down to you to ask this one question out of it all:

"What do you want"?

Before answering this huge question, take a moment to think. If whatever you *want* is not aimed at anyone else, if it is not taking from others, nor "evening the score" on someone, then fine. Yes, you deserve every good thing you can amass in life. As long as you are not living an empty or shallow life, then you deserve to have good in your life before you die.

Want to know what *I* want? It took me a long time to see it, but I know what *I* want now.

*I* want to live a life with purpose. *I* want to live my life for the purposes of furthering my biological input in life with a good message to those who follow. *I* see the truth about life in a linear way. You see, right now a 10 year old child now holds more knowledge in their hands with a smart-phone than that all of the humans on this planet did while living in the year 500 A.D....

My one lingering hope is that I left a message worth sharing beyond my lifetime. I do not need riches and social status for my life message to be done well. I just need to share as much of my self as possible with the world in a way that insulates me from what I failed at before. I need to go forth with a purposeful meaning by offering my writing and speaking in favor of good things in life.

"Good" is the longest lingering message we can leave to one another. We go from believing in fairy tales as children, to our believing in the stars or heaven as adults that will somehow save us from death being "final", all in the very same manner. So yes *good* is the strongest image we hold throughout life.

I believe that any hate you hold is self contrived and is biologically against everything you are designed for in life so much so I am betting all that I hold dear on it as my way to survive.

Just as surely as we create our own misery mentally, so too do we create our own healing.

Once I had this figured out, I took it as a personal challenge to be one of the most graceful at practicing this in my daily life.

See, it really does come down to perspectives and wants. If you can be truly honest and face your life with no bullshit, no con game for even yourself, you don't suffer mentally. You can get right on with your life and do what you want while being free of the yesterdays' sorrow. You just have to let go of your cheap ego and sense of humiliation or hurt that you contrived and use on your own life tools to stop it.

I never thought my ego was so real that it would trick me. I never knew the only way to beating your ego came from just being *nice,* as this is the one thing it was telling me not to do.

All along I see that my efforts to see myself clearly are also directly related to what I feel about other people's view of me.

I know now how to not be tarnished from others views of me. Want to know how come I believe this? Because I am the one *living example* that another person's view of who you are is truly meaningless in harmful ways. I swear now that some of the very same people who once thought I was a despicable murderous fiend, now also think that I am one of the most inspirational people whom they could meet in life. The very same ones. I tell you that I have actually met some of them and heard it from their mouth.

So who's perspective was it that mattered then, when I was being put down by these people? Or is it now, when they treat me with deference?

I honestly feel as if I am the one person who does not care  about any view that is not in sync with how I see myself from having this one unique experience. I get it. I go on, "they" fade away in time. I am left with my own perspectives to place on it all.

## Living the message you believe in.

I want to make it clear that I see myself as *not* being any kind of a "life coach". I do not want to be anything other than someone just like you, someone who has been trying to find a skill to rely on just to handle life. Many of the people who read this work are far more clever than I am, hold many more distinguished levels of education, or have completed more rungs of achievements than I have or ever will.

None of that matters really, as it is so true that you can learn at least *one* thing from any human on this planet. I happened upon a level of healing from a mindset that was totally unrelated to the outcome of it in terms of my outlook now.

I was bright enough to learn through further efforts of reading about Neuro Plasticity to see that my actions put me at the forefront of a new science aimed at helping humans.

"Neuro Plasticity" was as alien to me 10 years ago, as much as was the laptop to a caveman, and I concede that right now.

I was trying to re-acclimate to society. I was trying to handle my own internal struggles just by giving myself a break and being nice to my self. I was not driven to dedicate my life to a "philosophy" as taught to me by another life coach. I applied a very persistent effort to being nice and polite and kind mannered as the base tools of self healing. That is it.

No more is needed, nor can I say it enough that this is *all* that have I used as my "life skills" or tactics employed to not suffer more than I can help it.

I thus have to say now that I offer no overall meditation-based, nor any kind of some "word-driven-mantra" to follow.

I am not telling others about a new prayer-ritualized set of steps to follow for a feeling of nirvana. I am not giving you "12-steps" to anything, nor showing you "10-things-to-do" as practices to format into your life.

You and I are both biological beings with very set designs in our brain that we can enhance by simply tapping into our intrinsic energy. How this is achieved is done in many varying forms.

Our brain gets the same rewards from enjoying music, to praying, or just simply laughter. So there, they *all* work. How can I be your life coach if I am in need of the same things you are craving? This is the one reason that I felt like I could write this book. I am not trying to be anyone's "guru", life coach or any of that stuff.

I get to simply say:

*"I figured out a way that works for me to not be bitter, to not be bothered over things. And I ask, do you want to try and not be angry like me"? "If so, this is what I found out from trying this"...*

The one perspective that makes you the strongest is the way you see yourself as you interact with others. WHO you see yourself as sets the stage for all that you get in these rewards that I wrote of. It is all from the actions you put out, not anyone else.

This one area helps me, like others, to master social skills to the point of feeding off of your graceful intermingling.

It's like feeling as if you are skating in perfection while you are in a crowd, all for how you can go from one circle of humans to another one in gracefulness.

As you go from one group to another in positivism, you get caught up in how each set of humans offers you delightful treats for your being so alive to them all.

What I want you the reader to focus on is how your daily acts can be shaped into a sort of super defense system to feelings of being empty. You can work each day to be in a position to handle all of those hard moments you are yet to face with an ability you never felt you owed.

You can really re-tool your way of thinking when approaching things in the past for how they twisted you up inside from doing this as well. You can make yourself actually shape a new outlook for how you do not set yourself up with expectations for other human actions, simply when yours are foremost in mind.

The thing that fascinates me is that I never went in for all of this stuff.

I never thought for a second that if I went out of my way, striving to be nice, that I was anything other than a  pushover. I really did feel like everyone else does, in that I had to fight back to have my positions or feelings validated by other humans.

I could not stand it when others took me for a fool and all of it made me so willing to respond and struggle. I never in my life would have ever believed that now, I shrug off such thoughts for the waste of time that they are to me.

I literally smile now, when in the past I would have made sure I got my words in, or I made my righteous words and even my violence be validated.

I actually now try to listen to myself as I reassure my own mind internally of how "This is the same soup that I was served before, it is now just being presented to me in a different bowl"...

I really mean it too. I was always the last person in the room to ever try to accept that if I was pious, how it was a real strength. I would never think that letting others go on with their bad deeds or acts was anything less than me letting myself down.

I used to think that I could never "forgive' someone because that would be so huge a deal for me. Now? Completely dismissing them from my life for any attachments I feel for them as little as possible is an act of being nice to myself I do gracefully. I sincerely do. I actually taught myself to think of how nice I am being to myself by just not having anything to say or do with someone.

Sadly many people have been conditioned to think that "blood ties" allow for others to carry out horrible acts on you, all with a free pass expected afterwards. This is one of the most toxic things we allow.

I think that there has be a respect factor to be laid down in your life based on who hurts your growth. This goes for friends *or* family.

This is not me advocating anyone trying to actively lose bonds with caring people. What I am addressing here, is how so many people have so much hurt and angst in their life only because they have a toxic relationship with someone.

If you have found yourself living in a situation which you know is hopeless and broken, then you owe it to yourself to cut it out of your life. The notion that you owe someone any things for being in their lives is the biggest hook which is sunk into us.

People act like you are expected to overlook having them do the most atrocious acts on you, all for the sake of a notion that they share an immediate blood tie to you. They feel that they are due some sort of exemption to your bonding with them in a relationship like that. No way.

I waited for over two decades to go back home to my family. I saw in a short time after this that the kindest act which I could do for them was for me to leave. It certainly was my own kindest act as I was stopping myself from having to play out what I knew was a situation that was too broken to fix. I was not in any way being selfish in my leaving. I had enough of an education in the filed of psychology that I saw all of the dysfunction that was plaguing my family in the aftermath of what was done to me. I was going to add to it and be consumed by it if I stayed.

Leaving did not mean that I was ostracizing myself and nor did it mean that I was not wanting all of the benefits of the bonding or rewards of family. I simply created my own network of loving and caring people to surround myself with, people who provide all of the best concepts of bonding that family means to us in society.

If I could leave my family after 23 years of fighting to get off of Death Row just to come home to be with them again, then anyone can see that regardless of what you are made to feel that you owe anyone, you really have the right to live in peace. If you are not the one who is hurting others, if you are not the person who has to inflict emotional damage on those around you, then you have the right to end all of that by leaving.

I honestly am going to be fair like this to my own prodigy in life. If you and I cannot get along, then go. Go and make sure that you replace my inadequate ability to bond with you with a better one. If I truly am a caring person, then surely this is my wish for you. At the same time, if you and I struggle to be in harmony, then accept my leaving as a grace for us both to be soothed by, not as some reason to hold angst against me later on.

Both of my biological brothers are dead. They each died sadly from abusing booze and hard drugs. Yet my replacements for them now in my life is through the really good efforts I now make with other men. I have some of the best male bonds that I could hope for today because of what I have given to them each in time and sincerity. I have also found the most loving bonds with females on a romantic or family level, also replacing what my own biological family was losing out on enjoying with me.

What you feel personally inside about this topic is wholly down to what has been imprinted on you in your development. It is all what you have been conditioned to accept.

Maybe you see my way of looking at this as being cold or able to detach a bit too easily. Maybe you think I do not understand your own personal situation. Maybe, or *just* maybe, none of that really matters.

Your own value system is the point here. If I know that just by being around someone is making my insides churn and I am then emotionally wrecking my life with stress, why do I have to suffer this way?

If you are allowing yourself to be tormented for the few morsels of affection you get or some contrived words you know to be false, then you really are your own worst foe. You are letting yourself be degraded to the point of your own health being ruined, all for some lame notion that someone has a *right* to act as they do.

No one can have a right to bad acts because they were born in the same clan. If someone claims to love you, then they would be the first ones saying farewell with a smile as you part ways. If not, they are just broken and not willing to care for anything other than what they were sadly conditioned to believe.

It is up to you to care enough about your own life to stop being made to feel all of these horrible feelings of guilt that are not real any way.

At the same time, if you are being treated with grace by others, really appreciate it. Throw yourself into it so that the negative people do not steal this feature from you. I really had to work hard at this so that I did not end up lamenting something that I was inflicting on others. I really think that if you cannot extricate yourself from a situation, you have to really try and make pseudo-replacements as best you can.

You owe it to yourself to cut out the ones hurting you and focus on the ones who make you grow in love.

Had I not done this, had I stayed in Philadelphia, my life was going to be chaos and painful without any of my own actions having much to add badly to it.

I would rather others do as I have, and find your own life elsewhere, to then build it up on your own. I would rather see this than see them drink to oblivion or just sadly exist in life.

I guess this whole thing comes down to the analogy of the game of chess. You can play to win and make every effort to outwit others to be stress free, you can play to a "draw" where you only let others in only so far...Or you can even a "stalemate" where neither side wants to make an effort and you quietly quit.

No matter what, we have to play this game if we are mobile and going to deal with other humans in life. That is just how it is.

If you can set aside winning or losing for the clever ability to just play your own game, none of the negatives own you. If you and I played a game of chess and you won, my ego may make me want to try again. That's fine. But me? I want to think that I was thinking well past the obviousness of the game.

I want to be so enlightened that I instead focused on how my brain was being given this wonderful treat and all of it was down to me to enjoy.

This same perspective is applied to so many facets of your life if you think about it. We spend our lives dying poorly, or we spend it dying graceful and kind for knowing we have only one purpose in life. Please know that all I want is for anyone feeling like it is so unfair that someone else can make your life miserable is so wrong. How I handled it was to start anew with as much grace that I could muster. I have not always gotten it right and for that I feel silly. But knowing as I do now, I have found enough self respect to not repeat it poorly again.

I guess in the end, I really am living this message as much as any other right now and I have nothing but empathy for how you handle it your self.

# When you see the change in others.

I can state with a certainty that I have literally watched another person transform themselves directly as a result of my daily interactions with them. In the course of only one whole calendar year, I have witnessed my partner Laura change so diametrically from long held notions of her self or life so completely. This change in perspective and outward projections of herself are so evident in her reactions to things that most humans could not fathom handling.

I first began teaching Laura all that I knew about our biological drives that are implanted to us. Ones that are used in conjunction with pressures from society to then make us feel very much overshadowed.

I showed Laura how I faced this issue by being utterly pliant to the feelings this caused as I knew I had to experience it as we have all do.

What does that mean? Well whether or not you believe it, your body is in control of you and your identity that thing that you call your "personality" or "ID".

You were designed to further our species, period. You are endowed with a brain to help us find new solutions to our species. You are designed to produce children and bond emotionally. You got no say in any of your design and yet it is that last thing we want to admit is in charge. Me? I see that my wanting anything is all either an urge implanted within me or is one I made up of my own minds desire.

Now I know which ones are going to wreck my life if acted on them and I know the ones that are gifts to enhance me.

I also know that I should not be tormented over it all as I had no say in it's creation.

We love to smile at the poor hapless Salmon fish as it swims up-stream that one last time to mate and then die. We really do not in that moment see how we are no different in so many ways for how our body was designed. You can believe from a religiosity point of view that because we have been blessed with self awareness that we are separate from all other creatures. You can think that we are an evolved species put here by Gods, or whatever you want. The one truth is that you are going to get gray hair and your skin will shrivel and you will finally die just as you were designed.

What that tells me is that we should embrace our biological brain and body and stop letting so many social implants make you live with internal conflict ruling us. Women get put down for tight clothes and men are laughed at for flashy cars. Why do they do this then?

You are not only your own judge of what you know is right and wrong, but in truth you are truly the only person who can punish you for it.

You can get a beating physically, but in time it is only what you feel inside that matters to that memory. You can dismiss any notion of punishment for the realization that you could care less what they say as so many do, or you could take it all to heart and lash yourself endlessly.

"Addressing your biology" means you can find a way to not be tormented by what you do not have. Wanting children, wanting to feel truly that I am loved, while wanting to be given acknowledgment are all honest wants.

It is not having these things that makes us really mindful of how to effectively handle them. I know that I am a biological being who wants to further my species by wanting to pass on all of my knowledge and the good views of life I found.

I am hoping to be smart enough to take from this awareness all of the very best principals of bonding and developing the next generation. It allows me to not see myself as living my current life for my own needs. The world does not end when I die, yet so many of us live exactly this way. We forget that our gift of being giving a life to live is so that we can give the next generation a chance to find our answers. We are living at odds with biology when we do not do this.

So I taught Laura how I am dedicating my life to the awareness that I have a set time of living. That I am meant to further everyone who comes along after I die with my life now. I made her stop worrying that she was nearing the end of her reproductive cycle, that it is no different than when she entered puberty. I further taught Laura that I extended this outlook of myself to how I was more than happy to accept her children of a previous bond and nourish them.

I was willing to go and do every dedicated act for her children in tribute to what I was given by Laura. I showed her that what matters most is that we try very valiantly to pass on whatever good we have, so that we strengthen the next generations. The good I pass on to children will be their own gift to many long past my life.

Any hurt or pain can last only as long as that person wants it to be shared, just as any really decent thing you offer becomes their idealism and actions. I love that notion because even if I were to die before I finish this book, I still know in my heart that the efforts I have made with many will make them embrace every good I held myself up to them as being in my life.

This message to Laura went directly towards her self image of loving herself. The hardest thing for a female is to not be affected by the widely ranging effects of producing three children.

For Laura, who is only five foot, and one inch tall, childbirth is an enormous stress on the body. It also leaves after affects that are deeply challenging to her and other women.

Once I got Laura to really appreciate herself in a biological sense, she started to fall in love with her body, as her body was so in love with mine. She felt her body come to life for being entwined in mine because in unison like this, she was freely emotionally loving me. This triggered the wonderful biological gift that our bodies have to harmoniously sync up with others. Our bodies have this amazing ability to crave another being. We embrace this further in our emotive acts of adoration and we see this as love's divine gift.

And if you can embrace your body being in love with another it teaches you how to actually love your own body for giving you this unbelievable reward. That's what I showed Laura was real. We then tapped into this deeply.

In one year, a person who once could never accept so much about herself has been just so forgiving and so healing towards her own self. Laura is doing this for just having a new perspective about her biological designs and rewards.

I next began working with Laura to have her understand how she possessed all of this healing if she tapped into being nice to herself. That instead of past ways of being hard on herself, she could mend things with a softer approach.

Right before her eyes I handled numerous situations with others acting poorly in my life, and each time I dealt with it without angst she saw how I was sparing myself those feelings *she* would be consumed by. When she saw me face people who lied or took advantage of me, and I took every opportunity to rise above it, *she* then made the effort and was sincerely better for it.

Soon she was exorcising all sorts of toxic relationships from her life while she was also not affected by her own tormented thoughts by others.

Knowing that she was a good person, knowing that she was a decent and loving person who deserved respect and consideration also meant that she could base all reactions back to that one point. If she really is a nice person then she should respond to the negatives without being sucked dry emotionally. Yes, it stings to have things done to us in bad deeds, but I taught Laura to have the mindset of;

'Fine, you act low towards me today...just be consistent and act this way always, as anything else is a falsity I do not fall prey to'.

That way, she learned how to dismiss any act done. She could then set herself up to not be lured into further hurt by simply having a way of seeing herself as always being consistent. I consistently acted this way for her too.

Whatever another person does to me I cannot control. I just ask that they try to not fool themselves by then changing their act to pretend that is not who they really are. It's just that simple.

As far as your own healing when it comes to physical pain...

I have 11 broken bones that were never given a chance to heal which causes me tremendous pain levels. I have just so many reasons to allow my hurts or pain to make me easily lash out or make others know my pain. I never do this because instead of being tormented by my pain, I learned how to separate that from my interactions with others. In fact, I apologize to others for having to witness my pain and I hope I do not cause them too much discomfort for having to witness it. In this one kind way, I actually turn my suffering into a brain healing exercise that is helping me alleviate my condition.

Lastly, I taught Laura how respect drives love and respect is the true foundation of bonding. We are biologically drawn to pair up and loving efforts are meant to keep us together for our species to renew itself. I get that. But the thing that really keeps us together is respect.

This act that is intrinsic to our nature from simply a respect for things that can kill us, to those that can quench our thirst, we have a "respect factor" built in. Having respect for another human in a real effort makes every loving act so much more meaningful. I won't eat my food until I know my partner's food is okay. I won't talk over my partner because I can. I won't physically dominate and I won't emotionally bully because I really have so much respect for her. When you hold respect, you act so differently than at any other time with people.

Once Laura was given her respect, she then flourished and was comfortable being herself.

Laura was finally free to be the most comfortable version of her self in front of me. She was openly invited by me to treat herself as she would her best friends in life. In turn she allowed me to have all of her personality shine through as never before.

Laura did it all because she wanted to feed off of the good that this type of bond can offer. She did all of this amazing self healing and determined effort to grow on her own. All I did was offer nurturing love and as much respect as she could ever want.

All the while I amazingly fed off of this bond too and I also managed to produce all sorts of positive work for it. I was further allowed to heal with wonderful bonds with new children. In each way that I gave of myself in time and effort, I am witnessing all of the spread of good that is driven by my efforts.

Just seeing this in the results with her daughters or Laura has made me really tap into one thing really. I want the change that I see in others to not only be visible to me, but I want them to see it as they are doing it daily.

Without a bit of exaggeration, this one person very close to me is the example best shown to date, who can profess how they took to heart all that I had to grow so much so quickly.

It was Laura herself who then added to what I had taught her in so many fine ways.

In one year, this one person decided to tap into trying to heal their life by simply not reacting to the stresses others cause them. All to which allowed them the mindset to expound beyond it. Brilliant.

Laura has taken all of the tools she held all along within her and she used them. This, along with a new perspective of being kind to herself, rocketed her towards a better living quality.

The end result is having such a new way of living that Laura wants to teach others all about what she now holds dearly from it all.

This is what encourages me so much. If in only one year's time, this person who never before thought in these terms has shown such a remarkable change, then why would I believe she is the only one who can do this? If I can change her life, someone can and does change my own as well. I accept this right off as well. I am as much student in need as the teacher in all ways.

I am shaped by my own want to adhere to the finest lessons that I have learned from others. So, I am just now doing the same for Laura what was done for me. She is the one who then shares it with her lineage. My reward is seeing now her children be better humans and Laura a very fine example of women who I am so drawn to in respectful ways.

# The Charisma Effect ...

My partner Laura's development in a daily prideful manner was easy to show how my efforts in an intensive way helped her tap into so much inner strength. I have also seen this effect on a lot of others who spend time absorbing this outpouring of my emotive caring. Yet the one effect most apparent or noteworthy is the way in which I have what many call "The Nick Yarris effect" on humans. This comes in the first five minutes of speaking to me personally, or in large gathered groups while I am speaking to many.

My Spiritual Adviser in life these days Jivi Singh, is always cautioning me to be aware of my intense nature and how some people just cannot handle so much of me at once.

I really want to show here in this moment that all I am really doing is putting out all of this energy in the most genteel way. And yet, it is a tsunami to people who are not very experienced in life, or they are a bit aloof to such things. I get it. I have literally seen humans weep, nervously shift about in dismay, or just stand stunned in realizations of what I spoke of before them.

So what is **that**? I am just a man like any other. I have no skills as a trained actor. I am doing nothing more than just pouring out sincere words in the hopes that as others hear me in full. I see that all along I am still having one long conversation with my self. If you ever listen to yourself speak while yet going forward speaking to others, you know you have a further awareness of how those words are so YOU. So I *am* the kind salutations and wonderfully sweet endearments I speak. I am what I say so profoundly in this way.

I am as much in turn hit by my own "Nick Yarris effect" as I absorb all of this energy in turn from others while I try to be what I speak of.

The mannerisms are genuine that I try to carry myself with and that shines through in ways no actor can ever emulate. It is such a grace incorporated way of just tuning out all of the rest and just catching all of these vibes from people. Topped off as you offer a real effort to emote and share your essence in this very clever way.

During the 3 years which I spent reading each of the world's religions while incarcerated, I learned a fascinating thing. It was about Sanskrit. It was that the language was not aimed at the descriptive way other languages are that drew me to this. Objects are not described plainly in this language, they are words contrived of the feelings for them.

I learned that what you say in the *delivery* of your words is as important to the cogent subject matter they hold. I knew that I had managed to develop an adult mannerism of speaking in a difficult but rewarding manner that makes my voice softened. I saw that like speaking in Sanskrit, I was emoting in harmony with what I was saying in an innocent manner to myself in prison. One act from that time that I can not shake now is how I speak so delicately of words. What a gift to my charisma I had no idea was there.

I know my life hit a brick wall at age 20 when I was first placed into prison. I will always be boyish from this event and this shines through in my way of interacting with others.

I took all of the gifts of learning how to comfort myself while enduring torture, by speaking calmly to my own image as a way to soothe hurts, to transitioning it to my every day mannerisms.

Sorry that mine had to be so dramatic, but anyone can do this. My trick? Simply taking a single image that you like of yourself and then speaking as beautifully to that image as you can. If you suffer from public speaking fears, start by realizing that you are really just talking to yourself in life. All you need to do is speak beautifully to your own self first.

Your own self belief is evident to all and if you hold a self respect for yourself that also really shines brightly. Then there are the unique life experiences we each live and what comes of it all is charisma.

What you then do with this is all down to you. I acknowledge that I am one of the most charismatic men you can meet today because I really live in each of my days all of the ways that I project myself doing for others. I live as I act and in doing so my biology is in harmony with my brain that is free to thrive.

You cannot fake charisma and if you struggle to have an effect on others, don't bother worrying about it. You either will find it, or you just simply miss it at times. As long as you try, you are in essence better for it all, just because you at least get it enough to try.

I have a "Nick Yarris" effect on others. I love it that I do. I am having the same charismatic effect on others that I get from those who inspire me to tap into what *they* are about. If you can look at it in terms of energy, this is all being passed about all day in every form of media we share. Positive energy should be embraced in any way we can absorb it and we should try so hard to spread it.

I am as enthralled with the speaking ability and charisma of hearing Bruce Springsteen during his acceptance speech at the Oscars in Hollywood as anyone who is affected by my speaking.

I love it that we can be able to really produce wonderful moments between us with only words and expressions. All of it is this massive replenishing of our minds and central to our development. I am seeing this as I write it down as my own motivation to truly tap into every bit of this message with renewed vigor. I want to push myself to see how truly beautiful that I am able to make myself. I want to feel that I am indeed a really beautiful man for all of the ways that I go about being so meticulous in my kind ways.

I am really going to dedicate an effort from here on to stick to my moral code. I will always keep my word to others in respect. I have a bond with Laura and we each have a set agreement which all centers around one thing: Respect that is driven by love. NO bullshit. We just get it. I won't ever be one to crush her trust in my word to her, nor will she let me down as well. That now is my word to you as well.

As you absorb my message that I share in this work, please know that it is such an eye opener to me about how I need to now, more than *ever,* just take every bit of this to heart.

This book is not anything to do with what was done poorly to me in life as some way of leading readers on a journey in a tale told. This is where I am stepping out on a platform to say that what I have learned from so many others has completely changed me for the better and "here is why"...

To be fair, from here on I better walk the walk of a man who is trying to inspire others to put a real value on their words. I am bound definitively to my own promises to myself that this is who I am.

After all, show me someone who says "I swear I won't let *myself* down" and I will show you someone who I want to believe.

I am not letting anyone else down, I am letting *me* down in the worst way if my word is nothing but lies. That is why I try hard to always work so hard to show others how important my word to them really is.

In the end, I believe what makes me have an affect on others is derived from within them. They have this same built in want of being brightened up for human examples like mine that brings out their finest traits or qualities. I really believe that so often people want very much to show their own internal good. This *good* can only be set free from a leading example before them that I appear as.

I go forth believing that I am indeed lighting up the room with my energy. This is felt by those who want to be doing the same thing and I know it. I am as swept up in my own effect as any and I love how smoothly I have transitioned it into how I conduct myself around others.

I am not just into some form of self belief or really mindful of all that stuff, I just know that when I put it out there, my brain just expounds infinitely with growth. The rest of it is my own delightful introspective awareness of how I can then play with my gifts.

## Harder than life, kinder than love.

Since the day that I walked out of prison I was met with a very real challenge related to forgiveness and kindness both. I had no choice but to accept the kindness of anyone who was willing to help me. I also had to accept the act of forgiveness as a survival tool. I had no choice either way, so it was really down to me how to see this challenge.

For me to get out and then go and seek revenge or to make others pay for what was done to me was so stupid. I would have to live my life with them still very much in it that way. Since I never was a killer to begin with, why bother now, is what I thought about it all.

When my mother was telling me to be kind, she had a reminder for me about this as well.

The point of view that my mother had was that if I could wake up and be absolutely sure that every person whom I ever wronged had forgiven me fully, *then* I could consider being angry. She said that no matter what, that at some point I was overlooking my own previous acts while being the worst hypocrite acting angrily as I did so.

It is so true that we as humans can overlook all of our own deeds, to then point out others and make ourselves feel righteous when we are no better. Maybe I am blessed with having such a huge amount of things which I can never feel like others have or *will* forgive me for, that this lets me stay away from being such a hypocrite. Maybe this does allow me a helpful way to not being one to seek paybacks. I am really glad it is a feature of my life that I try to expound upon in words and deeds both now.

Long before I wrote this book I began trying to think of my efforts to have my life free of these two biggest challenges we face personally.

The two biggest things which we struggle with are: 1). Our sense of worth reflecting back to us from those we are personally connected to, or; 2). The need to appease our ego.

When we struggle to be validated by someone and are hurt by them, we are so angered for how our image before them is tarnished. That is when we find ourselves wanting to have our words or our thoughts be known, period.

When we find ourselves in the aftermath of someone doing wrong to us, our ego is set upon having us react and respond and we have to make sure we get ours in...then we explode.

I hate this last one most as it is like a drug. I have seen people become drunk with rage or their brains frazzled from anger.

If you watch, there are times when anger can be spread between humans like a sickness or disease. Like drugged animals it can be a shared experience. These two aspects of humanity are the true challenge we all face. What can you do about? If I told you to simply calm down you would most likely scream of scoff at me. Yet, that is the answer. A battle with anger by anger can never be won. But tell someone the alternative and they scoff and snort and or scream at you. Okay ego, wanna see how clever I am? You get no say any longer and I am going to sweetly tell you how much you lose this round as I rise above it.

Am I gifted solely for having lived in a conditioned environment for over 20 years that made me respect things most fail to? Am I at an advantage over others for having this conditioned environment from prison life present me with an ability that others lack out here in society? I do not think so.

I started reading about how others viewed kindness and anger. I also wanted to read about what others said about how they lived post-events of having terrible things done to them.

This is what I found out from my efforts...

Studies done on people who donate organs show that for the most part, they are no different than others in their communities. They mostly wanted to do an act of selflessness for a sense of betterment for themselves. They were doing an act that most of us view as a bit mad because of having surgery done to you. Yet the donors say they wanted to feel like their life had purpose.

What I was intrigued by was how this one article from the New York Post online showed how recipients of the organs and their families all shared a sense of love for the organ donor. They as well reported how they loved the organ now within the patient who's life was saved.

Why were people doing an act of kindness that most people viewed this act as something really risky or something they would not have the guts to do themselves. All the while they are mostly making the organ donor feel in self doubt at the same time.

Meanwhile the donor has little chance to use this act as a way to personally connect with the patient as this dynamic is removed by the medical system.

I then started looking at this study on how people who share genetic traits are drawn to one another in social activities. CNN News had this fascinating article in 2015 about how so many humans with alike genes come together in events held world-wide.

For the past few years since reading this article, this one piece about how humans who share genetic traits gather has really affected me mentally. I like this notion that I am drawn to others in one way.

It really seems to me like I have this huge "Empathy Gene" within my core make up. I honestly believe that I am drawn deeply to other humans who exhibit this same gene. We are the humans who can emote kindness without falsity. We are intrinsically sympathetic in our actions which come naturally to us. We are the humans who are able to make another person feel so vitally important, all for simple acts that we do for them as part of our make up as humans.

Am I blessed with this genetic code that has a heightened trait that allows me an extraordinary gift? Or have I just tried valiantly to tap into this trait we all share as best that I am able to?

Either way this is what brought Robin Sharma to me. It is what brought me to Laura as well. Is it what has drawn me to you or you to me?

Maybe all of the ones in life that we as humans revere all had that really great ability to tap into their empathy gene and this showed?

Whether it be Christ, The Buddha, Abraham, Muhammad, or Mother Theresa, were they not all examples of our most empathetic humanity?

I like to think that I do indeed have this wonderful genetic trait. I want to deeply nourish this gift for how it brings about all of this healing in life. I want to believe that we are indeed given a code of design no differently than that Salmon fish we smile at as it passes upstream to a grand finale of death.

As a member of this species I am given a wonderful gift that is only worth anything for how well I use it before I die. My gift to life is already built into me and all I need to do is use it.

Give a man like me who has had eons of time to contemplate things like this a chance to consider what to do with this knowledge, and I saw a way to use all of this in a genius way.

I saw that if I could try and override my ego and a sense of personally satisfying some draconian need to hurt others for what was done to me, that I was free to nurture me genetic and biological desires. I was able to apply the "Charisma Affect" to my own life knowing that I have a right to believe in what I am. All this is doing is believing in my design. What? I am not supposed to shine because some event blinded me overall in the past? Not a chance.

I feel like I am indeed blessed with a built in ability to become harder than life in this way. And yet all the while I am remaining kinder than love to others. Who says that you do not have this set of gifts that only need to be acted upon to create this wonderful bloom in your life? I believe in this so much that this is how I see the projection of my life playing out.

It all goes into my want to tap into kindness on that *next* level, and then the "next" one after that, as I feed off of my own genetic gifts.

I think that our environment plays a huge factor in many things which we are shaped by. Just like anyone else accepts this, yes I too accept it. But I also now believe that if you try and draw yourself towards your most beautiful traits as a human, (that you also can further this with your personality traits) to project a really stunning display of who you are. If I remove all of the ego driven traits, or dim them well, I am then contrasting this with a very determined effort to throw charismatic efforts into it all. I am then using every biological implanted gift for making myself a unique personality free of vulgarity.

I am accepting then that I am as beautifully designed or flawed without it meaning that I am lowered by it. I am instead tapping into what is best for my ability to swim as far up this stream of life we are all on, and do so with a great message for those who follow me.

I want to go as far as I can in life and bring with me all that I am, just like we all want.

I want then to have my message and my efforts in my own life to be a strength to those whom I bond with.

How does that make me any kind of gifted person that any other is not? And if this is true, then anyone who adopts this basic perspective of their life can be just a content as I am to not feel any need for vengeance. Forgiveness is a boring thought to all when you see well past this point to what lies ahead of you without it.

I keep saying it in this way so that people can grasp it...maybe I need a better formula.

To me, my telling folks how I see myself as being "Harder than Life, while being Kinder than Love" should be enough. If you can see yourself as being both of these things, then surely you are declaring that you know what it takes to hold onto each equally.

Doing this act in balance in life takes a lot of guts and I think this is what they may struggle with. Maybe they are not getting it yet that whether or not you like it, you have no choice but to try and be harder in the face of life's tough and dirty times.

Oh we all know as well how hard it is to be kinder than love itself. That would mean we could be sweeter than all that we were ever given and that is enormous.

I do not have all of the answers. I have so much myself to learn, so how could I say now that I am completely knowledgeable of this balancing act of life we all do?

All I know is that with the advancement of science lately, that I am aware that my path chosen in life to be utterly and meticulously polite are making me one of the foremost examples of Neuro Plasticity healing. I excel where others have not and it has led many to wonder what has brought this about most.

I am claiming now no special gifts and I am not even formally educated, so how could I master this field from that perspective?

The thing most relevant here is that for whatever reason that brought me to a certain set of daily practices that are invigorating my mind, I am making me live so sweetly in the face of what looks to others like overwhelming sets of sorrow filled events. If these practices have produced within me a wonderful persona, then why is not something you as well can achieve? I clearly am no different than you in make up or design. All I did was really believe in myself like no other could. I then employed one hell of an education to fully appreciate it all.

It all comes down to what you want doesn't it?

When we get to this last chapter to follow this one, (Sorry but this book need not be very long to convey my message) try remember this:

When I share what others have to say for my actions in their life or from my story being known to them, their *own* actions after this has all drove what happened within them. I did little more than awaken within them a trait they held.

I merely provoked others in life to use their own tools to a better perspective or a deeper appreciation of what they held all along. So are they not the same as me or even better? They just do not know what the Kindness Approach does to their brains in a rejuvenating sense as I do. Now have read about it I truly get it. Others who have not found out about Neuro Plasticity just know that it feels good to make others see how much they have empathetic genes which shine brightly within them.

When others call me inspirational or they tell me how my story has affected them deeply, I am reminded that this is why I could never call myself a "Life Coach". By the very definition of those words I fail to be one. I am not a manager of life. No one can manage your life for you. You have to become harder than life and work to educate yourself, Period. Then you have to address love with the most respect you can muster.

Anyone tells you that they can show you how to be like them is telling you how to not be like *you*.

# Inspirational intuition.

I am going to share the responses I have gotten from others in life that are due to my art (either in the form of my books or film) being shared with them, or my speaking before them affecting their lives. I want to show how this kind of kindness exchange is where all of my strengths emerge from. I want others to see what lies at the end of a the process of putting forth an effort as I have done, to lead your life in a kind manner. I want to show how that invites rewarding responses like mine.

I remember seeing Nelson Mandela being released from his prison custody time. I then saw how he went to work doing good. It was for me, the first instance of my being truly inspired by another human being.

I learned how he did the one thing that really opened my eyes to how he had a self perspective.

Nelson Mandela was given a platform well before he stepped out of prison from his education like I had. He chose to turn towards healing and then he set about trying to make a positive impact on life.

To me the message was clear and easy for me to follow. All I had to do was adopt this same perspective that whatever my past was, my present allowed for me to focus on doing good deeds. The rest of it is all so much an effort to deal with ego driven acts that I have no time for. I am not in need of governing a people to a new future as president as Nelson did.

I simply need to adapt the same posture of how my acts now truly override all of my yesterdays. All for how I am willing to do every thing that I am able to do in positivism now.

When I saw myself willing to act and construct my overall approach to what Nelson was doing, I also saw that because I was also given a platform like his, that others would see in me differently.

What I saw of humans that is to me intuitively inspirational is now what they see in me. In the past 13 years of life I have been the person whom others have been drawn to for how I have not taken everything "super personally".

It is from this perspective that I am truly tested to hold onto what I have shown of my life to people. In my own way I am bound to so many others because I convinced them that if they acted as I do, then they would be better for it in life.

I cannot step out in life on a huge platform directly claiming that I hold a relevant message that is applicable to many and then quit. I can no more turn and a year from now act all destroyed or broken for some mishap in life.

I am not allowed to get into a fistfight over stupidity nor be besot with booze in public acting foolishly. I am not permitted to launch vulgar attacks on the web and I am certainly not allowed to act boastful or too full of myself in public.

I can not be common in bad deeds or words because I made myself believe what I asked others to accept of me. I made myself believe that I really am a wonderful man who exudes genuine kindness. I am in my own reflection of others all that I want them to believe. The closer humans are in my life they are more and more reassured that I am indeed this remarkable man who has nothing but good to offer. I feed off of my being an inspiration to others like no other because I figured it all out.

I *am* every thing I want most to be known for from nothing more than my own actions. People in my life get the one constant that I always have been to them and it shines back .

I offer myself to them the most wonderful reflection of who I am. Oh what a wonderful gift that life has given to me wherein I can connect with others on this level. I adopt this posture that "walking the walk" is being simply your true self each day.

A shining sweet moment of thought for me is that as I made myself into what I want most to be. I found out that there is both a grace and an art to accepting others viewing me as part of their inspiration in life. Yes I accept that I am one of the strongest humans ever now. All for my capabilities to absorb so much chaos in life and yet project a sincere development of positive afterwards. That is remarkable for any of us to do. The level to which I have done it is surely enhanced for my charismatic application of my own persona. So yes, I am indeed a remarkable example of this wonderful message humans hold for one another in our ability to overcome hardship.

I emulate all of the finest qualities that we want to find within ourselves when faced with adversity and I project all of the best post-trauma behavior they hope to show the world.

In accepting this making an inspiration from others gracefully I try to always do one thing: I share how they are pointing towards the very same attributes of kindness or strength that I am to them.

And now that I see how my doing this in such an artistic flare of a manner makes me appreciate the exchange on my own level even more: I see all of this platitude driven encounter to be my healing. I am absorbing all of these wonderful accolades while also returning this grace in sincerity. I see how it is making me exponentially become this very thing to my own self as I do it.

I sit here now sharing all of this and for the life of me. it took me *years* to really appreciate many of the facets to what I what I just wrote.

We as humans want very much to feel our best qualities in life come to the forefront of our actions. We want to show our best when it most shows who we are to others. We want to share our kind deeds and be also lifted for knowing others appreciate what we had to get beyond in life to now just be happy.

How any of this became such a playground for my personality to come to life is just as much amazing even unto my own self. And all for how I can see my effect on my life and others with my own way of being sweet mannered.

I sincerely believe that most people can tap into their  intuitive ability to be inspired by or inspire others. just for how it then makes us into this person who is expunging all that they once were lacking.

I love it that in this way I am not the messenger so much as I am another person who has tapped into the message.

Looking at it this way I am no more relevant to your mental health today, as you are in charge of it is now for how you use me or others to grow.

So read the following messages to follow and as you do, please know that my responses to them really did not matter here. In each instance, these are humans who are showing what they are responding to in me is very much what they are most wanting to be. I love it that I am instrument which they heard their own best message within, and then they expressed all the good they are to me for it.

Here goes...

Hi Mr. Yarris, I don't know why I'm writing you bit I feel like I can't go to bed without sending you a quick message. I briefly watched the documentary that my girlfriend was watching called "The Fear of 13".

I just wanted to say thanks for telling this story of yours and I'm excited to watch this by myself tomorrow morning. I'm a veteran of the Iraq/Afghanistan war and I'm medically retired from multiple IED explosions resulting in TBI and the loss of both of my legs 6" below my knees. I'll keep this short since I'm not sure if I'll get a response or not. How did you push yourself every day? How did you not go crazy and give up when you wanted to so bad? Thanks for reading this.

   *When I think of how this man has so wanted me or anyone like me to be able to evoke such sentiment I am emboldened*.

Hi Nick, I just finished reading your book and was profoundly moved by your story.
I really admire the ability that you found within yourself to keep hope alive and your never-ending desire to be a better person.

What initially drew me into the book and kept me reading was the terrible sequence of events that dictated your life, your stories of the prison conditions and what day to day life was like for you.

However, the final few chapters in the book were truly an eye opener.

Although what happened to you was extremely unfair, unjust and cruel, you managed to rise above it all. But more than that, you managed to use those circumstances to become the person you are today - very few people manage to take the negatives in their lives and turn them into positives.

I can understand you not wanting people to feel sorry for you, as it was not entirely a negative experience. You would not have been who you are now without having experienced those things. That is an opinion I share about life.

I truly wish you all the best for your life, and your family.
I think people can learn a lot from you, not so much because you were a death row prisoner and all you went through, but because of your capacity to forgive, your ability to love without expectation and your deep insights about life.
  *This is what compels me to see how I have no choice but evermore be the man I presented myself as before them in written form.*


  You don't know me, nick.
But I have to say that you are an inspiration to me more than you will ever know.
It's very presumptuous to say that I'm proud of your courage, love of life and family. -But I am nonetheless.

I'll never be able to have the grace, wisdom and appreciation for life that you compared with me when I fill with air, I hug my twins, kiss my wife and walk into my job that you must have every day. But I will try.

I'm going to share with you my only real fear; The fear of outliving one of my beautiful twin boys. They are 9 years old. My sincere condolences to both of you. I wish I could help relieve the pain you both must fee. I feel bad when I prey that I will never have to know what you must feel now. For that I feel guilty.

Nick, your gift to me is your incredible resolve to continue the message that you have taught me. -And I guess for many others that can't communicate the message. I don't fully understand it all yet and its certainly a terrible burden you carry for me and your followers. For that I thank you.

That being said I hope I give you both some some comfort in the knowledge in that I won't take any day that I'm given in my life and my family for granted. I'm trying to live each day as though it's my last. Most importantly, you are a ghost that haunts me to remember what's important I hope don't disappoint you.
Thank you for your courage, inspiration and courage.
You are making a difference. I hope that helps and wish I could call you friend.

- *Friend? I call this family all day long...*

-

   DEAR NICK I have not long left an abusive relationship with the father of my child. Until I saw you speak live, until I heard your story, I was full of hatred. My emotions consumed me, I wanted him to pay for what he had done.

After hearing your story I realized I didn't have to feel that way, the actions of one horrific individual didn't have to destroy my life. I watched you lose everything that mattered to you, I saw you go through things that would ruin almost people. However you got through it, you came out the other side as a lovely, kind and caring person. I thank you for showing me other people's actions towards me do not have to shape who I become.

\*Every day others who are longing for the very same message I got from Nelson Mandela keep coming...

Nick. I just watched your movie.. and let me tell you. I am moved... I work as an officer previously at a prison and now at a jail.. being in these setting brought me in so close I believe.

I mean it brought me so close to your story that I am literally speechless.. that was so good. I'm so happy for the overturning of the case.. I'm sad you had to spend 20 years behind bars for a crime you didn't commit.. all in all, This was point blank amazing.. hope you are doing fine. Even though you might not respond.. just wanted to let you know that all those things.

*This makes me so grateful when an officer writes me.


DEAR NICK,
Been meaning to write a thank you for a long time now. I heard your story about last year; a point in my life where I was giving up on myself at every minor turn my life had to offer. Your resilience never came from a place of hate or anger.

No matter how much you seemed to be put in a place that was out of your control, you spoke of finding solutions through loving thought and hope. Most every morning I struggle to move not only from depression but injuries across my body including; dislocations of all major Joints, herniated disks: it's easy to be bitter about the pain, and project my suffering onto the world and others, which I'll admit I do often, but I refuse to stop what I love albeit I do take breaks. I feel your story is as much about your phenomenally unique journey, as it is about never closing your heart off to others. I'm not sure if everyone knows just how rare and difficult faith is to hold onto when facing a city-scape of adversity.

The morality and humanity of yourself, your other friends, and grinds who were/are incarcerated took center stage, and I believe that is the most admirable thing about having head such a compelling story.

Although the story was impart about your life, there was a genuine feeling that is was also about everyone you encountered along the way. I look back to your page for reference when I feel myself getting lost and treating others in a manner that doesn't respect my own being. Much love to Laura, and to you Nick - you've helped me and many others more than you could ever imagine.

*I sincerely get this person.*

So why is it then that disabled people, or people of so many walks of life that are making such a connection with me? I think it is this universal want that we all possess to express or adopt inspiration. I am to others either just a former screw up who went to jail and read some books, or I am something remarkable which we all want to be.

I have tapped into the fact that it is all of these people are using me for what they most want to find within. That this is making them have to hold onto this self image of who they want to be. That is why they reached out to me. That is what they are seeking an ability to hold onto from me to them project as well on others.

In seeing it this way I am so removed, and yet intrinsically linked to this spread of good that empowers us. To everyone whom I reach, whether it is in a market with my smiling polite face, or in my written work or professional efforts, it is always the same.

If this is so true of it all, then every average person can do what I am doing. I am seeking from others what I most what to be in life and I am taking on their messages as ones they have used to better who they are.

And in my doing so I am healing from my past, making myself deeper and stronger and all of it is then my effort to project it charismatically to the world.

Have you figured out how utterly simple this all is? You get from life what you put into it in this one unique way. That is the basis of making you like who you most are trying to be to others.

Intuitive behavior is linked so deeply to your perspective making. All you really need to do is make yourself into what you want to be by acting this way to yourself in front of others.

In the end, this is all that I have done.

## Living within my dying...

    I hope you can appreciate that I felt all along that this need not be a long work to convey the message of this book. I am so genuinely grateful that you took the time to share with me my hopeful attempts at sharing this work. I sincerely only want my life's story, and all that I have gone through up until now to hold meaning to me. I hope that it is a good message for what I try each day to do now.

    I want the same as you do. I want to demonstrate to *myself* that I am so worthy of what others feel for me today. I want to prove to myself what I am again and again in my deeds, not lame words. I want to feel good about myself for it and nothing more.

I am bound to you now that you read my words. I am no more able to change for writing this than saying my name at birth is not mine.

I think this is what holds people back from making an effort to believe in themselves. They do not want to be then tied to being this person constantly when inside they feel they are not. Me? I am going to keep right on presenting to others that this *is* who I am. I will bare the burden or delight in being this person consistently before them too. I am doing so because my loyalty to myself is not going to be cheaply held by me. No, I am going to embrace the fact that I chose to stand up and seek to be recognized. I am going to be fully aware of how this both affects me and others for what I am designed to do. Any fear of embracing this boldness is ego made or contrived fear. Neither will rule me and how I see my life.

This is the core of trying to really embrace my living while I know that I am dying each day. I feel this more than most because I was made to sit in a hour glass-like setting in a prison cell.

I was made to live in a way that made me feel like I was watching my life fade away as each day passed. This feeling has never left me and I try very valiantly each day to pay tribute to my own dying by being as alive to my life as I am able to grasp. I take that former torment of my life and I use it now in my life to cherish what I have.

I also am able to really appreciate how I am still living under a kind of a "Death Sentence" each day now just as I once did while in prison.

I saw once again that God has no favorites when our daughter Jaymie Leigh died. There was no one to blame or aim hate at. I saw how all along ever since my release, that I am the one driving how people see me or accept me.

I have no one to blame when this is gone wrong and humans see me in a poor light.

I get it, I am a dead man at some point. But after what I have been through, I also get it that I am going to fulfill my biological beauty in grace. I am going to do it with a mindful approach to living my remaining days to my own liking.

I am going to be bold and strong and willing to believe in the best of my features and qualities. I am going to ignore all the negatives from others because they are not living my life nor or they dictating it.

It is all so simple for me. All I have to do is go on being this wonderfully alive, sweet of nature man who exudes all the positive good within me. I am erasing all the hurtful meaningless stuff each day I do this well. I truly am free if I really am able to live without my past dominating me, nor my future ruined for how I cannot see past it all.

I want to be beautiful and I wish to be as graceful as I can to others. I want it for my own need to feel my life is as good as I can make it. How can anyone else deny this to me if it is meant as my own gift to myself? I don't care how many times I miss the chance to make this work for me. I know the times that it does work, how I get to be what I love most about myself. How can I be dissuaded from from doing this is when I know my rewards?

What brought you to me that is inside of you right now that you are responding to most?

Were you just curious, trying to see what makes me tick?

Do you honestly believe you got to be who you are if not for all the other humans you got your knowledge of life from?

Was it because you had to see what it is I could be wrong about?

What if I told you that none of that matters to me? What if I am proving to myself here in my writing that my design of this work was for my own healing? How about if it is true that it has very little to do with you at all? Would this make you less likely to embrace what I shared?

I was merely trying to fulfill a promise to my own mother that I would try to be a nice man who was always polite. In my singular efforts to do this I was awakened to the fact that I was using methodology that was the core of Neuro Plasticity. All I want now is for you to try my approach to life.

By happenstance I stumbled upon a mercurial way to rejuvenate my life and I also found a way to use a meticulous behavior to shape my every day life to one of feeling happy.

How or why you picked up this book then has to come back to you. What is you want to take from what I did and why I have done it all?

I know how to ignore my yesterdays that were so full of nasty rotten deeds done to me or done by me. I know that the only way to be content in life is to have none of it attach itself so deeply that it robs me of today.

I never expected that the answer to doing this was to simply to go around with a mindful effort of being kind. I never knew how this would heal it all. I was literally the last person in the room to ever see or believe this was my answer. And yet, if not for one request from my mother on one day in my life, all of this may have never been shaped as it has.

You need to make a promise to someone or yourself.

You need to be what I have felt that I need to be for another. What I have known and learned is one big lie if every good person is fake.

You need to show me that people like Mandela was wrong to get out and show a very positive and good nature to the world.

You have to convince me that a paraplegic who is never given my chances in life but smiles none the less to others in life is wrong.

I thought I was clever because I knew what made the wind blow on our planet. Ask people about this very simple thing which they can actually see moving the leaves on trees or push bits of debris across the road. They are stumped to tell you what causes the wind.

I learned that it was actually our Sun that is heating the air around the equator of the Earth that is then smashing up against the polar air at the top and bottom of the planet which makes constant wind.

When I figured out that what makes me super strong in life is actually my *kindness*, I was even more astounded to hold this knowledge than I was about knowing what makes the wind blow.

The fact that I have used so much grace and individual charm to make this effort of mine a remarkable example to others is what makes me write this book. I am actually feeding off of the very things that I am sharing with you because I see myself able to do this like few can.

My way of living has made me accept myself as being one of the most loving and caring humans one can meet in life. I liken it this way:

I was once a remarkably gifted athlete. Blessed with good genes, standing over six feet tall, I had a flare and style to my athletic ability in sports. I most likely could have played a professional sport to a very high level.

It does not matter that I never got to be this in life except for how I can still recall the trill of knowing I had that *gift*. I can still feel the moment mentally when I could run without effort and simply 'glide".

I feel like I have now awakened this other prowess of a gift that makes me glide just as gracefully as I once did on the field of play. I am able to do effortlessly what a lot of others struggle with.

The singular greatest fear in life is said to be public speaking before large crowds. The self image of our faltering is what drives that. Me? I love the way in which I can take this shared fear and turn it into my greatest attribute. I place myself into this with all the vigor and energy that I want to take back from this act. I have not one single fear of faltering because I am so gracefully gifted by my own actions *before I spoke*, that I flawlessly handle it.

I know that being awakened to my dying is changing my every action. I see how little time that I have left to make my message to others be heard. I am like every other person in that I am shaped by this singular want.

I am saying now that it is down to you, not me, to make up your own lasting message. Irony here is that I now see how this book is exactly like my own prepared speech for my execution.

All of my efforts to master language and be able to speak came from one desire that I had on Death Row. I knew that I was in a hopeless situation wherein I was going to be executed. So, I threw myself into having the acumen to speak with dictum while they took my life. I worked tirelessly to have a prepared speech which I could say without faltering.

This longing that I had was so deeply ingrained within me. I overcame my own trepidation, a severe brain injury, as well as a scrambled mind from drugs and booze, just to hold myself together and speak beautifully one last time. Imagine how you would want your last words to be on a date  that you know is your last day to live. What would you say?

For me it came down to wanting to show the world that I was no more important and yet no less beautiful than a neutrino emanating from the Sun. One that is passing straight through all that we think is solid or formidable. I wanted to show kindness to those taking my life and show moreover that I had found a way to love myself before I died.

I drove myself into the belief that I could lay calmly on a medical table and have them poison me to death. I was going to use that moment to show all who cared that I was loving and decent.

As the drugs would fill my blood and kill me, I was going to be my own most loving self for the act that my message which I shared was far more important than that of the events leading to my dying.

This effort from my previous life of being told that I would be indeed put to death makes me able to appreciate things few can.

I see now that this writing of my ending to this book is indeed my life's statement to you all. I may not have chains on me and intravenous drugs being pumped into me this day, but I am sharing with you what makes me say:

"I am like you. I am a human being with a biological design that features an ability to share with you both empathy and love. I am blessed in my life to have found a way to like who I hold myself to be, and I am genuinely kind to others. I offer you my respectful and polite greetings while I sincerely wish you good in your life before you die. I hope too that we each fulfill our efforts to make our species that much brighter and better for what we have done in our lifetime".

"As we pass through life we belong to one another and we have no choice but to remain bonded as isolation taught me that without humans I am not a human. Without others I am no one and in this way I cannot ever quit life".

"My last lingering hope will be that you read my words and you took to heart the very same message that I have"...

You are my inspiration. You who read this and nodded in appreciation for my knowing what *you* intrinsically know is right makes *me* feel so alive. I spent so many days trying to figure out a way to answer the simple question about why I am not angry. Although the answer seems just as simple I like it that no matter what, my taking the KINDNESS APPROACH has made me the happiest man I ever felt to be in life.

I want to thank you for being the answer to my own needs. I mean it. I sat here imaging you, hoping that you were like me in all of the best ways. I want you to be proud of yourself for how you are so much like me. I want to know that what I wrote makes us each feel like the only true way to appreciate our drying is how graciously we try to live life in all the most invigorating ways we are meant to.

If we never meet then I send you my love, respect and hopes for you to be happy in life. I will try my best always to represent for you what I have held myself out to be in this work. I will strive to make you feel a fondness for me like no other because I honestly want this from you. I want to feel good for being a nice man who is polite, so all I have to say is..."Thank you and I am very grateful for *your* kindness".

With love always,

Nick

## Author's note and acknowledgments.

I did my best to try and take some terrible circumstances and change for the better. When Robin Sharma wrote to me and told me how much he appreciated my efforts I then learned from him the answer to what I was doing. I like it that his compliment became my understanding in this way. My hope is that I can continue to emulate all of the best features we have as humans. I just want to have meaning to my life in this way.

This book would not have been possible without so many others who showed me what my kindness meant to them. I see as I close out this work that I have so much to learn and do before I stop. I am only 55 and I cannot possibly be wise enough to know all of what I should do from here. I got a plan.

My plan is to work hard and earn enough to retire as a school teacher. Yes, I would like to finally get credentials, teach a social studies course, and give my time to public service. If I never make it to this goal I at least take delight in knowing my dream is not self centered. I want to be a father and husband and fulfill my biological design beautifully alive to love.

The rest is trying to live well while having the terminal illness of "time". I am watching for my end to come with a grace born of knowing that this was all meant to be.

Thank you especially to Laura Thompson. It was her words that gave me the idea to write this book. It was her words that became the summation. It was her love that makes me so believe in myself as well. I admire who you are to others now. I see you going on and doing what makes you so special in life as no other. I could not be more proud of you honey.

That's it. Bye and I love you all.

Printed in Great Britain
by Amazon